PETER

Susan Martins Miller

Illustrated by
Ken Save

A Barbour Book

© MCMXCIV by Barbour & Company, Inc.

ISBN 1-55748-659-X

Published by Barbour & Company, Inc.
          P.O. Box 719
          Uhrichsville, Ohio 44683
          http://www.barbourbooks.com

ecpa Member of the
Evangelical Christian
Publishers Association

Printed in the United States of America.

PETER

"NO, I'M NOT AFRAID OF DYING"

CHAPTER 1

"Are you afraid of dying?"

The young man, his eyes dark and intense, finally asked the question that had been on his mind for weeks. He had just barely gotten inside the door before the question tumbled off his tongue. But he could not wait any longer. This old man faced death; everyone knew that. Yet he did not appear disturbed by what lay ahead of him. Day after day he sat in the sparse Roman room, peacefully praying and humming. He hardly seemed to notice the young man's presence.

"Please, sir, answer my question," the young man pleaded.

In response, the old man turned and looked at him with raised eyebrows. "Afraid of dying?" He shook his gray head. His curly beard wagged from side to side. "No, I'm not afraid of dying. Why should I be?"

PETER

The younger man, hardly more than a boy, had been bringing food to Peter, the prisoner, for six weeks. He set down the tray he had carried into the house that evening on the table before the old man. Beside it he set a jug of liquid.

"No one wants to die," the young man argued.

"True enough," Peter agreed, "but that is not the same as being afraid of dying. What have we got for the evening meal tonight?" He lifted the lid off one container and sniffed the aroma of broiled meat. "Meat again. I was hoping for fish." Another motion of his wrinkled arm revealed freshly baked bread. He smiled with pleasure. "Ah, the bread is still warm."

Peter's behavior only puzzled the young man further. How could this prisoner, who was surely going to be executed within the next few days, s[.] peacefully inquire about his food and deny that h[.] was afraid to die? He glanced toward the door thinking of the guard on the other side. Peter was no

"MEAT AGAIN. I WAS HOPING FOR FISH"

a dangerous criminal. The young man speculated that Peter was probably not even capable of hurting anyone. Yet he had angered the emperor of Rome by something he had said and now sat in a Roman prison awaiting his sentence.

"Why did you come to Rome?" the young man blurted out.

Peter sat at the table with his eyes closed. His lips moved ever so slightly as he prayed over his food. His eyes opened. "I came to Rome because God told me to come here." He stabbed at the meat with a knife.

"But if you had not come to Rome, you would not be a prisoner now."

Peter shook his head. "This is not the first time I have been a prisoner. If I made all my decisions based on whether I would be in danger, I would have accomplished nothing in my life." He poured some liquid into a cup and washed down the chunk of meat.

"WHY DID YOU COME TO ROME?"

PETER

"Then how do you decide what to do?" the young man persisted.

Peter laughed robustly. "I've done a lot of stupid things in my life."

"Like what?"

"I chopped off a man's ear once, a soldier with a dozen companions ready to strike back."

The boy's eyes widened.

"I tried to walk on water. I lied to protect my own skin, denying everything I believed in. I can't tell you how many times I acted before I thought. And it got me in trouble every time."

"But they say you are a leader."

"Yes, they do. And I am." Peter agreed as he tore off a piece of soft bread. "But even leaders make mistakes, don't you think?" He sat back in his chair and considered the young servant, whose eyes met his stare without hesitation. Obviously, the younger man wanted Peter to continue, to tell the whole story.

HE SAT BACK AND CONSIDERED THE YOUNG SERVANT

PETER

Peter put the bread in his mouth and started chewing. "Will you be in trouble if you do not return soon?"

"I don't think they will miss me tonight," the young man replied.

"Well, then, let me try to answer your questions more completely."

The young man moved across the room and sat on the edge of the bed, opposite Peter.

"Tell me why you really came to Rome."

"Because God told me to," Peter repeated. "The believers here started the church on their own, without the help of anyone who had known Jesus. I came to see what I could do to help them understand his teachings.

"So you are a believer of this . . . Jesus," the young man said quietly.

Peter took another swig of the liquid. "We were all skeptical at first. My brother, Andrew, and I were

partners in a commercial fishing business with another set of brothers, James and John. We had hear of this fellow Jesus many times. We had even heard him speak. Then one day, John and Andrew managed to spend a whole day with him, and life was never the same after that."

More questions filled the young man's eyes.

"Perhaps we should light a candle," Peter said, "and I will tell you the whole story."

"I WILL TELL YOU THE WHOLE STORY"

COMMERCIAL FISHING WAS HARD WORK

CHAPTER 2

The day had been long with little to show for it. On the only decent catch of the day the net had ripped violently. Simon had stood in the boat, disgusted, as most of the fish slithered away. The next several hours had been spent making the repairs that would let the business partners keep fishing.

The tanned, muscular man in his mid-thirties sat in his boat at the edge of the lake. The Sea of Galilee was an immense body of water fourteen miles long and six miles wide. He loved this lake upon which he had spent his life. Commercial fishing was hard work. He and his partners could be out on the lake in the beating sun for hours at a time with no fish in their nets. But when a good catch finally came, it was worth the wait. The four partners—two pairs of brothers—were making a good living for their families.

PETER

Today he had been waiting alone. His brother, Andrew, had disappeared early in the day with one of their partners, John. James was missing, too. From time to time, Simon lifted his eyes to the road leading down to the lake, hoping to see Andrew coming back to work. The sun rose higher and higher in the sky. Peter moved the torn net in his lap to repair another spot and started to grumble under his breath. "You'd better have a terrific excuse for leaving me like this."

At last he saw Andrew coming. Turning his attention back to the repair, Simon worked more intensely. There was still time to go back out on the lake and try again if he had some help.

"Andrew, come and help. The net's torn again."

"Never mind the net, Simon."

"Have you lost your mind? We need this net or we're out of business."

"Simon! You must come and meet Jesus."

"NEVER MIND THE NET, SIMON"

PETER

Simon tugged on the knot in the fishing net one last time to make sure the repair was secure. He looked up at his brother, Andrew, and squinted into the sun behind him. "You've been with Jesus?" He had stood in the crowds and listened as Jesus spoke on several occasions. Jesus talked eloquently of the coming kingdom of God and preached the need for repentance by the people.

"John and I spent the day with him," Andrew explained. "Simon, I am convinced that he is the Christ. He is the Messiah we have been waiting for."

Andrew reached down and pulled the net away from his brother. "Come on, Simon. Put on some decent clothes and come and meet him."

"There's a lot of work to do here," Simon protested.

"Aren't you listening, Peter? I said I found the Messiah. Come on!"

Soon Simon saw for himself. He stood with his

"ARE YOU LISTENING, PETER? I FOUND THE MESSIAH!"

brother, Andrew, before Jesus.

"I have brought my brother to meet you," Andrew explained.

Jesus looked at Simon intently. "You are Simon, son of John. From now on you will be called Peter, the rock."

"What does he mean by calling me the rock?" Peter asked his brother later as they walked away from Jesus. "Everyone can see that we are fishermen."

"I saw the way he looked at you," Andrew said. "Perhaps he sees something in you that you do not see in yourself."

Peter stopped and looked back toward this stranger who had seemed to look right through him. Their meeting had been casual. Jesus met dozens of people every day. Why did Peter have the feeling that this was different?

"Hurry, Andrew," Peter urged. "We've got to get

"YOU WILL BE CALLED PETER, THE ROCK!"

these fish to the market before the stalls open up. Skillfully, he pulled a fish out of the net and tossed it into a sack in the bottom of the boat. "I don't want to miss the busy hours. This is too good a catch to let spoil because we got there late."

"I'm working as fast as I can," Andrew said, adding a pair of fish to the pile. He looked over at their partners. "Looks like John and James did well today, too. They have their father and some hired men helping them."

"All the better for all of us." Peter tied the top of the sack closed and heaved it over his shoulder. "I'll take this first load. You come with the rest as soon as you can."

"I'll be there in a few minutes. But why don't we let the net down once more to see what we might catch while we're gone."

Peter put the sack down and reached for one end of the now-empty net. "Careful, don't get it tangled."

"I'LL TAKE THIS LOAD FIRST"

PETER

With experienced movements, the pair let the circular net down into the shallow water on one side of the boat.

"That should hold till we get back," Peter said. He turned to pick up his sack once again.

"Simon, look! Behind you!"

Peter turned quickly, slightly alarmed at the tone of Andrew's voice.

"Jesus?" he asked, though it was obvious who was standing on the shore near their boat.

"Peter, Andrew, I hoped I would find you here."

Peter spoke matter-of-factly. "We're here every morning at this time. We're fishermen, and this is where the fish are."

Jesus looked at them thoughtfully. "Come, follow me," he said, "and I will make you fishers of men."

Peter looked over his shoulder at the sack of fish he still held. It was a good haul, representing hours of early morning work. It would be foolish to

"JESUS?"

abandon it at this point.

Andrew was already moving out of the boat to follow Jesus up the beach. Peter set his load down and followed, too. *What does he mean, fishers of men?* he wondered as he quickened his step to keep up with Jesus and Andrew.

They did not go far. The next stop Jesus made was at their partners' boat. James and John were getting ready to let their nets down again, but Jesus spoke quietly to them for a few minutes and they soon climbed out of their boat and left their haul to the care of their father, Zebedee.

All four partners now stood on the beach with Jesus, not sure what their next step was. They would fish again on another day, Peter knew. But today would be a day they would all remember; the day they had entered into a new partnership.

Jesus turned to the small group of men who had left their nets to follow him. "We will go to

WHAT DOES HE MEAN, FISHER OF MEN?

Capernaum for the Sabbath."

I would go anywhere for this man, Peter thought. *I would do anything that he asked me to do.*

I WOULD GO ANYWHERE FOR THIS MAN

"BUT...ONE LITTLE BOY'S LUNCH-?"

CHAPTER 3

"How in the world did you find that little boy with his lunch?"

Peter heaved on an oar as he sat across from his brother.

"Jesus said to go find food," Andrew answered, "so I did."

"But one little boy's lunch—who could have imagined that Jesus could feed five thousand people with two fish and five small loaves of bread?"

It was late in the evening. Peter, Andrew and ten other men whom Jesus had called to be his special followers were out in a boat on the middle of the lake. Several hours earlier, Jesus had sent them on ahead, planning to meet them later.

"Has anyone else noticed how windy it's getting?" asked Matthew. He gripped the side of the small craft with both hands, bracing for the next gust.

PETER

The fishermen among the group looked at each other and shrugged. "Sometimes the sea is like this," Peter said, unruffled by the way the boat was leaning to one side. "You're a tax collector, Matthew. You've spent too much time counting coins. We can manage." To prove his point, Peter leaned on the oar once more to stabilize the boat's motion.

"We've been drifting around out here for hours," James said. "Do you think Jesus is coming with us tonight, or should we go on ahead?"

"I think we should wait a little longer."

"But we can hardly see the shore as it is."

"He must have gone back up the mountain to pray."

Each of the twelve disciples had an opinion about whether they should cross the lake and wait for Jesus on the other side, in Bethsaida, or continue drifting until he was ready to join them in the boat.

"It's been a long day," said a voice at the back of

"YOU'VE SPENT TOO MUCH TIME COUNTING COINS"

the boat. "As long as we're out here, I'm going to try to get a little sleep."

"Go ahead," Peter said. "The rest of you relax, too. I'll keep watch."

Most of the men settled in and tried to get comfortable in the wooden boat. An extra cloak served as a pillow for one or two, but most had nothing with them except what they wore. Their feet were dusty from spending the day on the mountainside, and they were exhausted from carrying baskets of food to five thousand people—and collecting the leftovers after everyone had eaten. They sprawled out from the front of the boat to the back and gave in to their weariness.

John and Andrew stayed awake with Peter. They murmured softly to each other about the miracle they had witnessed earlier in the day and their recent experiences on the preaching trips they had taken in pairs.

THE MEN SETTLED IN AND TRIED TO GET COMFORTABLE

PETER

"Peter," John said after a while. "The wind is really picking up. This is rough water, even for fishermen."

As if following John's instructions, the boat lurched to one side and water sloshed in, waking several sleeping disciples.

"What's wrong?" came a startled cry.

"Everything is under control." Peter and Andrew sat across from each other working the oars. The boat seemed to steady.

Peter started to give directions to some of the others. But his words were lost in the howling wind. Soon everyone was awake, scrambling to hang on to something.

"We're going to turn over any minute now!" someone yelled.

Even Peter could offer no words of encouragement now. Tipping over and spilling into the sea was very likely. The wind gusted again, pushing them

"WE'RE GOING TO TURN OVER ANY MINUTE NOW!"

farther off course. His full attention was focused on keeping the boat upright, with the help of several others who had joined him at the oars. He hated to admit that his muscles were starting to ache from the continuous effort. He felt as if he were pushing against the entire sea with every stroke he made.

They had been on the lake all night and dawn would be breaking soon. At least then they would be able to see something. Right now, they battled the darkness as much as the wind.

Suddenly, several disciples jerked back from the side of the boat.

"What is it?" Peter demanded, sensing their fear.

"There's something out there."

"What do you mean?"

"I don't know. But something is there. It's a spirit of some sort."

Fear rippled through the entire group and a collective moan rose up against the wind.

"THERE'S SOMETHING OUT THERE !"

"You're imagining things," Peter insisted, sounding irritated. "Or dreaming."

"No! Something is out there!"

Whatever was on the sea was coming closer. They heard a voice.

"Have courage. It is me. Do not fear."

The words were nearly blown away in the torrent of air swirling around the boat. But Peter recognized that voice.

Still fighting the wind, Peter peered into the darkness. It was as if he were looking into a black hole. But gradually his eyes focused and he discovered the form of Jesus standing on the water not far from the boat.

"Lord," Peter called out, "if that is really you, tell me to come to you on the water."

For just a split second there was silence. Then the voice said, "Come."

Peter dropped his oar and stood up roughly,

HE DISCOVERED JESUS STANDING ON THE WATER

rocking the boat.

"What are you doing, Peter?" the others demanded.

"That's Jesus out there," he answered. "I'm going to Jesus."

"Peter, come to your senses," they pleaded.

But it was too late. He ignored their warnings and climbed over the men in his way. Within only a few seconds, Peter had stepped out of the boat and onto the water. He put one foot in front of the other, taking a step, then another, then another. Breathlessly, he walked on the water toward the voice that had called him. He was walking toward Jesus.

The wind howled around him. As his clothing flapped behind him and the current of air blew past his face, his eyes seemed to open anew. He was walking on water. This was impossible!

At that moment he began to sink. When he tried to take another step, rather than hitting a solid floor of

HE WAS WALKING TOWARD JESUS!

water as he had the moment before, his foot went right through the wave and pulled him off balance.

Peter sank below the water line rapidly. Thrashing his arms, he managed to pull his head above the water and gasp for air.

"Lord!" he tried to say, but his mouth filled with water. He spat it out and ducked the next wave. "Lord, save me!" Peter cried out, with his arm stretched upward. He could see Jesus clearly now.

Just before he sank once again, he felt the strong hand of Jesus grasping his and pulling him up to safety.

"Peter, why did you doubt?" Jesus asked.

Together they tumbled over the side of the boat into the arms of the waiting disciples. Instantly, the wind quieted and the sea was calm.

Someone wrapped a blanket around Peter's shoulders. His chest heaving as he gasped for air, Peter looked around him. Dawn was breaking in the east.

"PETER...WHY DID YOU DOUBT ?"

PETER

Jesus had settled into the middle of the boat, assuring the disciples that they were safe. The boat rocked gently, lapping against the rippling water that only minutes ago had been turbulently stirred up by a fierce wind storm.

Why did I doubt? he wondered to himself. *This man is the Son of God.*

THIS MAN IS THE SON OF GOD !

THE HILL HAD TURNED INTO A MOUNTAIN

CHAPTER 4

The mountain loomed before them like an enormous dirt tower. Peter glanced over at John and saw that he was sweating, too.

When Jesus had said that he wanted to get away from the crowds to pray, it had been nothing new. Peter was used to the way Jesus would find a quiet spot to sit with some of the disciples to talk and pray. Feeling restless, Peter had liked the idea of getting some exercise. Along with James and John, Peter had followed Jesus as he started to walk up the hillside.

But the hill had turned into a mountain. They passed several places suitable for quiet prayer. Higher and higher above the town the disciples climbed. Peter's legs were aching and he needed to stop and take a deep breath. He and John had been glancing at each other, both wanting to stop, while James hiked ahead of them with Jesus.

Finally Jesus stopped. "We can rest here for a while," he said.

They had come to a flat spot with a small clearing nearly at the peak of the mountain.

Peter dropped to the ground immediately, convinced that his legs could not have gone another step. "Lord, why have we come all the way up here?"

"To pray," Jesus answered simply.

"Couldn't we have prayed in town?"

"Stop complaining, Peter. You'll feel better in a few minutes." Jesus moved across the small clearing and sat down on a low, flat rock. His head was already bowed in prayer. Apparently he was not going to say anything more about the hike up the mountain.

Peter inspected the surroundings from the perspective of lying flat on his back on the ground. If Jesus wanted privacy, this was the place to come.

"STOP COMPLAINING, PETER"

PETER

Peter turned his head to see an animal dart into the bushes near his face.

James and John had chosen their places more carefully, sitting on rocks as Jesus had. But Peter had sprawled in the dirt, and now his arms and legs felt too heavy to try to move. He twitched his nose as a gnat flew into his eye. He knew he was supposed to be praying, but his mind was foggy from exhaustion. Maybe Jesus was right. Maybe if he just rested for a few minutes, he would feel better and then he could pray.

Peter closed his eyes and was asleep immediately.

The sudden light frightened him. Though his eyes had flown open, Peter thought he must still be dreaming. He rubbed his eyes with his fingers, ignoring the dirt on his hand, trying to bring what he saw into focus. But it did not make sense. Surely he was dreaming.

THE SUDDEN LIGHT FRIGHTENED HIM

PETER

No, it could not be a dream. John and James had sprung to their feet and now stood beside him, seeing the same thing he saw.

Jesus stood before them, but not looking like the Jesus they knew and traveled with. His face was not a human face—it was more like a sun. With a gasp, Peter realized that the source of the light that had awakened him was Jesus' face. They could hardly even look at Jesus. His whole body had turned into a spinning tumult of light. His clothing was not clothing, but pure whiteness, whiter than snow, brighter than any light on the planet, blinding in its intensity.

Peter lifted a hand to shade his eyes. His heart beat loudly in his chest as he tried to make sense of what he saw. For a fleeting second he wondered what John and James were thinking, but he could not tear his attention away from the vision to speak to them. The three of them stood motionless, puzzled, terrified.

JESUS STOOD BEFORE THEM

PETER

He saw two men talking with Jesus—two men who had not come up the mountain with them. In fact, two men who had been dead for hundreds of years. Moses and Elijah, ancient prophets in Israel, spoke to Jesus. Peter could not hear everything they said, and much of what he heard he did not understand. They were saying something about Jesus' departure and how he would go to Jerusalem.

Peter shook his head. He did not understand any of this. How could this be happening? He had seen Jesus perform miracles before—heal sick people, cast out demons; even his own mother-in-law had been healed by Jesus. But this was different.

Moses and Elijah faded away. Jesus was once again alone on the mountain.

Peter gasped for air, suddenly realizing that he had been holding his breath ever since he had abruptly awakened. "Lord," he said, "it is good for us to be here. If you are willing, let us make three monuments,

MOSES AND ELIJAH SPOKE TO JESUS

one for you, one for Moses and one for Elijah."

Peter was not even sure what he was saying. Though the intensity of the light had passed and the mysterious visitors had disappeared, the experience would not be forgotten. It would not fade from his memory—it should not fade. Somehow this event, this vision of glory, should be remembered. Three monuments would remind him of this place and this experience of light.

But even as Peter spoke, the scene changed again. A bright cloud descended on the four men standing on the mountain and wrapped itself around them. Jesus, James, John and Peter were swallowed up in the light. Peter's eyes were squeezed shut. It was impossible to look into this light when he was standing in the middle of it. He was again holding his breath; he felt his heart straining against his chest. His sore legs and tired muscles were forgotten as terror immobilized him. What was happening? What

WHAT WAS HAPPENING?

was this all about?

At first he thought the sound he heard was thunder, but in a split second the low rumble became a voice. The cloud itself seemed to speak.

"This is my beloved son, in whom I have delighted. Listen to him."

Peter lost his balance then, frightened down to his very bones. He fell against James and then into John. All three of them tumbled to the ground with their faces in the dirt, terrified.

And then the voice stopped. And the light went away. And the mountain was quiet and peaceful once again.

Timidly, Peter opened his eyes and looked around. Gradually, he pulled himself up to a sitting position. James and John were doing the same. They looked around. There was no one there but Jesus, and he looked as he had always looked: an ordinary man wearing a simple robe and plain sandals, looking

"THIS IS MY BELOVED SON IN WHOM I HAVE DELIGHTED"

bedraggled the way most people would when they have climbed a mountain. Peter's chest heaved as he tried to catch his breath. His mind flooded with questions that he had no words for. He looked at John and James, who looked as confused as he felt.

Jesus stepped toward them and put his hand on Peter's shoulder. "Rise up," he said, "and don't be afraid."

Peter gulped. *Don't be afraid?* he asked himself silently. Was that even possible? He had stood on a mountain with the Son of God; he had seen Moses and Elijah; he had heard the voice of God himself.

Gradually his heart returned to its normal rate.

"Lord, we don't understand." Peter turned to see that John had been able to say what they were all thinking.

Jesus' answer was simple. "I will answer your questions on the way down the mountain."

"LORD, WE DON'T UNDERSTAND"

THE PASSOVER WAS BEGINNING

CHAPTER 5

Peter held on tightly to the bundle of food tucked under his arm as he wove his way through the crowd. He stopped abruptly to avoid knocking over a small child whizzing across the road as if the crowd were not there at all. Smiling slightly, Peter shook his head at the innocence of such a child.

For days the streets of Jerusalem had been crammed with people visiting from out of town—including Peter and the rest of the disciples who had traveled there with Jesus. The Passover holiday was beginning, and Jews from miles around had chosen to spend it in Jerusalem.

Ever since the weekend before, Peter had roamed the streets full of confidence and faith. The people of Jerusalem had hailed Jesus as a king as he rode into town on the back of a donkey, and the disciples had been proud to be his closest followers. After three

years of traveling around, preaching and fending off
the hostile religious leaders in many towns, at last it
appeared that they were getting the recognition they
deserved. Even if the leaders did not like Jesus, the
people clearly adored him.

"Blessed is the king who comes in the name of the
Lord!" they had cried out.

Three long years. Peter had no regrets about
becoming one of Jesus' followers. But he certainly
liked the idea that at last Jesus would be received by
the people as the king that he was.

The disciples had rented a room above a house so
that they could spend Passover together with Jesus.
Peter took the stairs two at a time and delivered the
parcel of food. The table was already set and most of
the food laid out. The room was filled with the
aroma of cooked lamb and warm, flat bread.

As the time for the meal arrived, all the disciples
gathered in the room, eager for the celebration that

THREE LONG YEARS

hung in the air around them. Their conversation buzzed in small clusters until it was time, at last, to begin eating.

Peter had hardly noticed how quiet Jesus had been when he first arrived. But now he watched with an unsettled feeling in his stomach as Jesus took a piece of bread, gave thanks to God for it, and then broke it. He spoke strange words.

"This is my body, which is given for you." And later, as he poured the wine, he said, "This cup is the blood of the new covenant, which is poured out for many."

Peter tilted his head thoughtfully and considered Jesus' words. For three years, Jesus had been speaking to them in mysteries. Sometimes he explained what he meant; sometimes he did not. Peter wished that Jesus would just speak plainly. Peter was a simple fisherman; he made a good living, but he was not highly educated. Most of the other disciples had

PETER CONSIDERED JESUS' WORDS

no more education than he did. So why didn't Jesus just say what he meant? What did he mean by all this? And why had he been telling the disciples that he would be leaving them soon?

When the meal was over, Peter was determined to get some answers to his questions. He knew the other disciples had some of the same questions; it would not matter if they overheard his conversation.

"Lord, where are you going?" Peter asked.

Jesus looked at Peter and was quiet for a moment before answering. "Where I am going, you cannot follow, but you shall follow me afterward."

Another mystery. What in the world was Jesus talking about? Peter fixed his eyes intently on Jesus, looking for any clue of meaning as Jesus continued talking.

"You disciples are the ones who have stayed with me in all my trials. As my father appointed me a kingdom, I am appointing you, so that you may eat

"YOU SHALL FOLLOW ME AFTERWARD"

and drink at my table in the Kingdom and may sit on thrones judging the twelve tribes of Israel."

Peter did not understand. Not a word of it. But one thing he knew was that he did not want to be separated from Jesus.

"Lord, why can't I follow you now?" he asked. "I will lay down my life for your sake. I will go anywhere with you."

Jesus smiled, but his face was sober. "Peter, will you really lay down your life for my sake?"

Peter held his expression and looked Jesus straight in the eye.

"Satan will try to deceive you," Jesus said. "He will try to shake your faith loose. But I have prayed for you, Peter, that your faith will not fail."

Peter stood up and moved closer to Jesus. The many mysterious things Jesus had been saying in the last few days flooded his mind. Whatever Jesus was talking about, Peter wanted to be with him.

"I WILL GO ANYWHERE WITH YOU"

"Lord, I am ready to go with you, both to prison and to death."

Jesus spoke quietly. Peter almost had to hold his breath to hear the low words. "Peter, before the rooster crows today, you will have denied me three times!"

The words stung. Peter had repeatedly pledged his love and loyalty to Jesus. How could Jesus think that he could possibly betray him or deny him? Hadn't he said he was willing to die for him?

Peter did not press the point with Jesus. But when Jesus said later that he was going to the Garden of Gethsemane to pray, Peter quickly agreed to go with him. This would be a chance to prove his loyalty and devotion. He would stay with Jesus no matter what happened.

Peter had a hard time staying awake as Jesus prayed. He scolded himself as he thought about the many

"YOU WILL HAVE DENIED ME THREE TIMES!"

other times he had fallen asleep while Jesus prayed. But he could not keep his eyes open, and three times he fell asleep. He was not alone. Most of the disciples had come to the Garden with Jesus, and everyone there had fallen asleep.

When Peter heard the clatter of the armor worn by Roman soldiers, he was instantly awake and alert. All the disciples were on their feet immediately, sensing the danger ahead.

An army official and a group of soldiers were followed by a swelling crowd who had come to see what all the commotion was about. Peter's hand went to his sword. If anyone meant to harm Jesus, he was ready to defend him, even if it meant his own death.

Out of the crowd stepped Judas, one of the disciples. Jesus stood very still as Judas stepped up to him and kissed him, identifying him clearly to the Roman soldiers. They had come to arrest him. Sud-

OUT OF THE CROWD STEPPED JUDAS

denly, it was clear that everything Jesus had been talking about was really going to happen. He was going to be taken away from them.

Some of the disciples moved closer to Jesus and spoke in a hush. "Lord, should we strike with our swords?"

But Peter was not waiting for instructions. He had made his decision. He drew his sword and with one swift motion sliced off the ear of the nearest soldier. Blood spurted out as the man screamed and dropped his own sword. Peter had his sword poised to strike anyone who might step forward toward Jesus.

Jesus' voice behind him was loud and firm. "No more of this!" To Peter's astonishment, Jesus touched the soldier's severed ear and instantly healed it.

After that, Jesus was seized by the soldiers with no further resistance. They led him away roughly, dragging him faster than he could walk. Peter trailed along in the crowd, blubbering his protests but

"NO MORE OF THIS!"

helpless to do anything for Jesus.

What puzzled him most was that Jesus accepted these events so peacefully. Surely he knew that they meant to hurt him.

They came to an intersection and the guards turned up a new street.

With a stone sinking in his stomach, Peter realized that Jesus was being taken to the high priest's house. This surely meant something terrible was about to happen.

SOMETHING TERRIBLE WAS ABOUT TO HAPPEN

HE HAD BECOME REALLY FRIGHTENED

CHAPTER 6

Shadows loomed all around him. Peter looked around the courtyard cautiously. He knew this was where the soldiers had brought Jesus—to see the high priest. Peter had followed Jesus from the Garden to this place. Through the streets of Jerusalem the growing crowd had moved, stirring up interest in every block.

At first Peter had protested the arrest of Jesus and run alongside the guards demanding that they release Jesus. But no one bothered to answer him, and that made him more frustrated and angry. And then he had started to be scared. Gradually he had fallen behind. Finally he was trailing at the edge of the crowd and for the first time that night he had become really frightened. If Jesus were put in prison—or even executed—what would that mean for the disciples and the other people who had followed Jesus during the last three years? Were they all in danger? Was he in danger himself?

As these questions filled his mind, Peter had let the distance between Jesus and him grow larger and larger. But he followed all the way to the high priest's house. John, he knew, had gone inside with Jesus. He had no idea where the other disciples had gone. If they were as frightened as he was, they would be smart to keep out of sight.

Peter was tempted to stay out of sight, too, but he had to know what was happening to Jesus. So he entered the courtyard outside the high priest's house quietly and nervously.

Shivering against the wind, he wrapped his extra cloak a little tighter. Peter stayed near the outer edge of the courtyard, watching everything around him. Guards, soldiers, and servants mixed with the curious street people who had followed Jesus to this place. The courtyard was busy, even though it wa

PETER STAYED NEAR THE OUTER EDGE OF THE COURTYARD

getting late, and the night was gripped by cold. Snippets of conversation drifted through the air and settled on Peter's ears.

"He's an insurgent. We had to arrest him before he started a revolution."

"He's just a Jewish carpenter with a few dozen followers. He's no danger. The Jews have so many religious leaders already. I don't understand why they think he's a threat."

"I just follow orders. My orders were to arrest Jesus of Nazareth, so I did." The soldier showed no concern for what would happen to Jesus.

Peter fumed inwardly. How could these Roman soldiers sit around a fire talking about Jesus as if he were just a public nuisance that had to be taken care of? To them, Jesus was just another part of their jobs. He glared at them angrily in the dark.

His eyes settled on their fire. It glowed a bright orange against the black sky, beckoning him toward

"I JUST FOLLOW ORDERS"

its warmth. His cloak was not protecting him against the biting wind. Perhaps he could just get close enough to warm up for a few minutes and then back away again. If anyone discovered him, he hated to think what might happen. But it was so cold. Once again he tried to wrap his cloak a little tighter.

Everyone was drifting toward the fire now. If Peter stayed on the outskirts, it might start to look suspicious. Grateful for an excuse to move toward the glowing warmth, he shuffled his sandaled feet away from the courtyard wall and toward the fire ring in the center. Without speaking, he settled down among the crowd and fixed his eyes on the fire.

A servant moved smoothly around the courtyard with mugs of warm liquid for the soldiers. Peter tried not to notice what she was doing, but each time she came near him, she seemed to pause and look at him for a few seconds. He avoided meeting her eyes. Once he even moved to the other side of the circle to

HE AVOIDED MEETING HER EYES

escape her scrutiny. But a few minutes later she followed him. Finally she sat down next to him. He could feel her stare burning into the side of his face.

"This man was with him," she announced to the crowd around them.

Peter felt the bottom of his stomach drop out. He heard the rustle of soldiers changing their position to look at him. He should never have come this close to the light of the fire! In the shadows against the wall no one could be sure who he was.

"Woman, I don't know him," he muttered, without moving his eyes away from the warming glow. To his relief, the moment passed. She moved on with her jug of hot liquid. No one seemed to have paid any attention to the servant. Why should they? Roman guards did not take advice from household servants.

But the crowd was made up of more than Roman soldiers. Cautiously, Peter looked around him to see what sort of people were curious about the fate of

"WOMAN, I DON'T KNOW HIM"

Jesus. He recognized very few people; Jesus' fol
lowers were not among the crowd. Suddenly Pete
felt overwhelmed at his stupidity in following Jesu
here. Why had he not gone wherever the othe
disciples were? Trying very hard not to look a
nervous as he felt, he glanced toward the doo
through which John and Jesus had gone.

A man sitting across the fire ring from Pete
finished gnawing the meat off a chicken bone an
tossed it into the fire. The bit of fat left on the bon
instantly sizzled and spit up steam. The man looke
at Peter, whose face was clearly lit by the fire.

"You are one of them," the man said.

Peter looked around. Some had heard the man'
accusations, but no one was reacting. Nevertheles
Peter wanted the man to quit staring at him.

"Man, I am not!" Peter emphatically denied an
relationship with Jesus. He tried his best to simpl
blend into the crowd.

"YOU ARE ONE OF THEM"

PETER

Peter looked away from the fire only to watch the door to the high priest's house. Jesus had been inside for hours, and Peter was getting more anxious by the moment. He tried not to look at the door too often, and when he did he tried to seem casual. Why didn't Jesus come out? Why didn't John at least come out and tell him what was going on?

For more than an another hour he sat by the fire and wrestled with these tormenting questions. Perhaps he should just leave. Surely the news would spread all over the city once Jesus came out. The decisions of the high priest were never secret for very long. In the meantime, Peter could be waiting somewhere much safer.

But he had waited this long. It might only be another few minutes. He spread his hands out toward the fire in front of him and held his palms up to the heat.

"Certainly this fellow was with him, for he is a

HE SPREAD HIS HANDS OUT TOWARD THE FIRE

Galilean." A man's voice jarred his thoughts, and instantly Peter realized the man was talking about him.

Peter pulled back from the fire. "I don't know what you're talking about. I don't know this man."

In the background a rooster crowed. Another day was beginning.

The clatter of chains told Peter that Jesus was finally being led out of the house and through the courtyard. He wheeled around and found himself staring into the eyes of Jesus.

And then he remembered what Jesus had said to him a few hours ago: "Before the rooster crows, you will disown me three times."

"...YOU WILL DISOWN ME THREE TIMES "

JESUS WAS CONDEMNED TO BE EXECUTED

Peter picked up a handful of sand and let it dribble through his fingers. He had been doing that all day, sometimes wondering if the sand was real, if he was real, if anything that had happened in the last few days was real.

After meeting Jesus' eyes in the high priest's courtyard and hearing the rooster crowing in the background, Peter had bolted away. After that, he kept his distance from Jesus. He knew what was happening. The whole city knew every detail of what happened. Urged by the Jewish leaders, crowds had stood in the street and screamed for Jesus' death. And the Roman ruler, Pontius Pilate, had done as they asked. Jesus was condemned to be executed by being nailed to a cross.

The only disciple to stay with Jesus throughout the trial, sentencing, and execution had been John.

PETER

Peter was afraid he would never recover from his shame at having denied knowing Jesus and abandoning him.

But things were different now.

"Has all this really happened?" he asked aloud, looking at the handful of disciples sitting with him on the beach. A lone candle set on an isolated rock in the middle of the circle lightened the faces of Peter's companions. "Has Jesus really come back to us? Or have I dreamed it all?"

"If it's a dream, then it's a powerful one," John said, "because I saw that empty grave, too. He wasn't there, Peter. He actually did rise from the dead."

"And we all saw him when he came through the wall of that room where we were hiding from the authorities," James added. "It's impossible that we would all imagine exactly the same thing."

"I can't make sense of any of this," Peter said,

"HAS JESUS REALLY COME BACK TO US?"

kicking the sand. "I never expected any of this to happen, and I don't understand what it means."

The other disciples nodded in agreement.

Peter raised his eyes to the sea. It was dark. He could hardly make out the water of the Sea of Tiberius against the night background. Every now and then a streak of moonlight caught the tip of a wave and made it shimmer.

Everything that he had devoted his life to for the last three years was turned upside down. Yes, Jesus had risen from the dead; yes, the disciples had seen him several times. But what did it all mean? What did the future hold? Peter had come to the beach to escape his unanswered questions, but the others had followed him there. Perhaps out on the lake he could be free of their weight for a few minutes.

"I'm going fishing," he announced and started walking toward his boat.

"Wait," someone called after him. "We'll all come."

"I'M GOING FISHING"

Peter sighed and then gestured that they should follow.

They fished all night. But they caught nothing. Not a single fish to distract them from the questions that plagued their minds.

Finally, early in the morning as the sun glimmered on the blue-green water, they headed toward shore.

"Peter," James said, "someone is trying to tell us something."

Peter put his hand against his forehead to shade the glare and looked toward the beach. A lone man stood there gesturing and calling out to them.

"Have you caught anything?" the man called out

"No!" Peter shouted back.

"Cast your net on the right side of the boat, an you will find some fish."

Peter turned to his companions. "Is he crazy? We've been out here all night. There aren't any fish

around here today."

But Nathanael and James had already started throwing the net out on the right side of the boat. Immediately it filled with fish. The weight of the net pulling on the boat made the small craft tilt to one side. The disciples scrambled to haul in their catch.

"It's too heavy," Andrew said. "We'll never get it in without ripping the net up and losing all the fish."

Peter started to go help with the heavy net. Suddenly John reached out and put his hand on Peter's arm, gripping it so hard it hurt. "Peter!" he said, "It is the Lord!"

Instantly Peter lost interest in the fish. He looked again at the beach and saw that John was right. Unable to stop the urge to jump, he did—right into the sea. With steady strokes he swam toward Jesus.

The other disciples followed with the boat, dragging the heavy net behind it.

Dripping, Peter stood up and waded the last few

" PETER ... IT IS THE LORD ! "

feet out of the water. Jesus had a fire going on th
beach, with some bread and fish. "Come and hav
breakfast," Jesus said. "You can bring some of th
fish you just caught."

Peter turned around and went to help with th
catch. As they pulled them out of the net and sorte
them, they counted a hundred and fifty-three fish

"This is an incredible catch!" Peter called ou
exuberantly. "Incredible. And the net didn't eve
tear." He scrambled back up the beach to the fire an
laid some fish on it.

They ate heartily.

Peter leaned back in the sand, satisfied. The catc
the breakfast, being with Jesus again—it all ma
Peter feel that perhaps his questions would be a
swered. Twice before Jesus had come to the di
ciples while they were behind a locked door. But th
time he had appeared out on the beach, whe

"COME AND HAVE BREAKFAST"

anyone might see them together. This was no dream, no figment of his imagination. It was really happening.

He turned his head and smiled as Jesus sat down in the sand next to him. "Did you have enough to eat?" Jesus asked.

Peter rubbed his stomach with one hand. "Enough to last me two days."

Jesus smiled. "I'm glad." After a moment of comfortable silence between them, Jesus spoke again.

"Peter, do you love me?"

Peter sat up and looked at Jesus. "Lord, you know I love you."

"Then feed my sheep."

Peter was not sure what Jesus meant. Another puzzle. He started to straighten out the tangled net. Jesus reached for the other side to help him.

"Peter, do you love me?"

"Lord, you know I love you."

" PETER, DO YOU LOVE ME ? "

"Feed my sheep."

What did Jesus mean—asking him the same question he had asked only a moment ago. Was there a different answer he wanted Peter to give?

Together they folded the circular net into a neat roll and stowed it in the boat.

"Peter, do you love me," Jesus asked again.

"Lord, you know I love you."

"Then feed my sheep." This time Jesus continued. "Let me tell you something, Peter. When you were younger, you got yourself dressed and you walked where you wanted to go. But when you are old, you will stretch out your hands and another will dress you and carry you."

Peter lifted his puzzled eyes and met Jesus' gaze. "Follow me," Jesus said, "follow me."

"FOLLOW ME...FOLLOW ME"

"HOW CAN I TALK ABOUT THINGS I DON'T UNDERSTAND?"

CHAPTER 8

"They want to hear you speak, Peter." Andrew urged his brother forward.

Peter resisted. "Me? Why me?" He looked around the room. Dozens of people watched his movements. He knew Andrew was right; they were expecting a speech from Peter.

"You told them before that the Scripture had to be fulfilled," Andrew said. "That's why Jesus died like he did, and why God raised him from the dead. They want to hear more."

"But there is so much that I don't understand," Peter protested. "How can I talk about things I don't understand?"

"I think you understand more than you realize you do." Andrew put his hand firmly on Peter's elbow and tugged. "Peter, you have a hundred and twenty people waiting to hear you talk. You have to say something."

PETER

"Not everyone here speaks the same language," Peter argued. "Many of them won't even understand me anyway."

Andrew gave Peter a look that he had seen all his life. It meant that his brother was not going to give up. Sometimes Andrew could be just as stubborn as Peter.

Peter looked around the large room and gulped. In the weeks since Jesus had risen from the dead, their group of 11 timid disciples had swelled to a hundred and twenty. They had outgrown their little upstairs room and started meeting near the temple. More people were joining them every day. Now that Jesus had returned to heaven, they needed a leader. But should it be Peter? Jesus' words to him on the beach echoed in his mind: "Peter, feed my sheep." Was this what Jesus meant?

He started to move toward the front of the room.

Suddenly an unearthly sound strained the corner:

HIS BROTHER WAS NOT GOING TO GIVE UP

of the building. Instinctively, Peter raised his arms to cover his ears with the palms of his hands. He could not help but cringe. It sounded like a violent wind blowing—but he felt no wind, only the thunderous, rolling sound. He felt the floor vibrating with the strange noise. Frantically, he looked around for some explanation, but there was none. He could see no possible source for this sound. It swelled until conversation was impossible. Everyone in the room stopped, frozen in their places and overwhelmed by the enormous sound.

Then something stranger still happened. Flashes of fire appeared in midair out of nothing at all. No one had lit any candles—it was still quite early in the morning. There was no fire for heat. But the flames were there, flashing in the air. Peter was ready to spring toward the door, to herd the crowd out to safety. But nothing burned. Instead, the fire seemed to separate and settle on each of the disciples. It

FLASHES OF FIRE APPEARED!

simply dissolved into their heads and shoulders.

Instantly, their silence was broken. But when they began talking again, it was in languages they had not spoken before, languages from all over the world.

As they spoke, they saw the heads of the crowd around them turning toward them in astonishment.

"Are these men all Galileans? How is it that each of us hears in his own language?"

The commotion had attracted an even larger crowd. People, hundreds of people from the street outside, pushed into the room till there was hardly room to stand.

"They are declaring the wonders of God in our languages!" they cried out.

Some of the people huddled in small groups, their faces full of bewilderment. "What does this mean?" they wondered.

Peter turned toward Andrew excitedly. "This is it, Andrew—the gift Jesus promised us, the gift he told

"THIS IS IT, ANDREW-THE GIFT JESUS PROMISED US"

us to wait for. The Holy Spirit has come on us."

Andrew's voice was urgent. "Peter, now it is more important than ever that you speak to the crowd. Say something."

Peter could no longer deny that something truly important was happening. He knew he had to say something. Grabbing a chair, he hopped up on it to get everyone's attention.

"Fellow Jews and all of you who live in Jerusalem," he began, "let me explain this to you. Listen carefully to what I say."

His heart pounded. What was he going to say next? How could he explain what he did not fully understand himself?

"People of Israel, Jesus of Nazareth was a man sent by God to you. Through him, God did miracles among you. It was God's purpose that he would be handed over to death on a cross. But God raised him from the dead. It was impossible for death to keep its

"THE HOLY SPIRIT HAS COME UPON US"

hold on him."

Peter scanned the crowd, looking for any sign th
they understood what he was saying. The wor
tumbled out of his mouth faster than he could thin
But as he spoke, he grew more and more confiden
It was as if God himself were speaking throu
Peter's words. He took a deep breath and continu

"Hundreds of years ago God promised King Dav
that he would place one of his descendants on t
throne. This was Jesus. God raised Jesus to life; w
have all been witnesses to that. Now he has pour
out the Holy Spirit on us. This is what you ha
heard and seen here today—the Holy Spirit h
come."

Peter's voice thundered boldly now. "Let ever
one in Israel know that Jesus is the true Lord a
Christ."

He paused and searched the crowd again. H
speech had attracted even more people. Hundre

"JESUS IS THE TRUE LORD AND CHRIST"

who could not fit in the room were pressed against the outside walls listening to him talk. Were they understanding? Should he say more?

"What should we do?" a voice called out from the middle of the crowd.

Peter answered immediately. "Repent. Be baptized. Every one of you. Be baptized in the name of Jesus Christ for the forgiveness of your sins. And you will receive the gift of the Holy Spirit."

Peter dropped down off the chair and put his hand on his brother's shoulders. "We must baptize these people, Andrew," he said. "We must go to the river and baptize anyone who believes."

Together they forged their way through the crowd pressing in on them. They gave instructions to the other disciples about their plan to lead the crowd to the river for baptisms.

"I'm so glad you decided to speak," Andrew told Peter.

"WE MUST BAPTIZE ANYONE WHO BELIEVES"

Peter nodded. "So am I. By the Lord's grace, will not stop speaking now."

Before the day was over, three thousand peopl had joined the group of believers. And when the da was over, Peter understood better what Jesus mear when he said, "Feed my sheep."

PETER UNDERSTOOD WHAT JESUS MEANT

"THERE HE IS AGAIN"

CHAPTER 9

"Come on, Peter," John said. "I'm ready to go to the temple."

Peter looked up from the parchment he had been writing on all morning. "Is it three o'clock already?"

"Just about. So let's get going."

Peter brushed off his cloak and ran his fingers through his beard. He was ready to go.

Side by side the two friends walked toward the temple to pray, as they did most days at this time of the afternoon. As they got closer to the temple, the crowd got thicker, not only with fellow worshipers but with beggars.

"There he is again," said John, pointing toward one beggar. The man's feet were twisted at strange angles, and his ankles stuck out in an odd way. Obviously it was impossible for him to walk. He was being carried into the temple by a couple of other men.

"He's here every day," Peter commented.

"And every day he wants money," John replied.

"Well, he's hardly in any condition to earn a living for himself."

John turned his palms up to show his empty hands. "I don't have anything to give him."

"I don't have any money, either," Peter said, "but if he asks us, we will give him something else."

They were near the temple gate. As they brushed past the man with the bent feet, he reached out for them. "Can you give me a coin? God will bless you if you give me a coin." It was the same thing he said to everybody every afternoon. His open hand was outstretched toward Peter and John, but his eyes were already roving to his next prospect.

Peter stopped abruptly to look at him. So did John. The man continued to look around the crowd.

"Look at us," Peter demanded firmly.

The man's friends set him down on the ground and

let him lean against them for support. He looked at
Peter, his eyes lighting up with the excitement of
getting money.

"I don't have any silver or gold," Peter said, "but
what I do have, I give to you." He stretched out and
took hold of the man's right hand. His voice rose
boldly, and he could see that many people had
stopped to watch this encounter. "In the name of
Jesus Christ of Nazareth, walk!"

Peter tugged on the man's hand, pulling him away
from the support of his friends. The man stood!

Peter's eyes dropped to the man's feet. The ugly
twisted feet and frail ankles looked completely normal.

The beggar timidly put one foot out in front of him
and let his weight fall on it. His hands were stretched
out, ready to break his fall. But he did not fall.
Instead he took another step, and then another. Next
he tried jumping. "Praise God! Praise God! This is a

"IN THE NAME OF JESUS CHRIST OF NAZARETH, WALK!"

greater gift than any money. Praise God!"

The crowd around the temple buzzed with excitement.

"This man has never been able to walk!"

"He's been sitting at this gate every day for years, begging."

"This is amazing! He is really healed!"

"Who are these men who did this?"

The man threw himself against Peter and John in gratitude, holding them tightly and saying over and over again, "Praise God."

People from all over the temple area and the surrounding streets were gathering to see for themselves that the man with the twisted feet had been healed.

Peter gently pried himself loose from the man's grasp and turned to face the crowd.

"Why does this surprise you?" he asked the crowd. "The God of Abraham, Isaac, and Jacob—the God

"PRAISE GOD!"

of our fathers—has glorified his servant, Jesus. You handed him over to be killed and disowned him. You killed the author of life, but God raised him from the dead, and we have seen that with our own eyes."

He looked around the crowd, knowing that he held their attention. The sight of the man jumping around was clear evidence of the importance of what had just happened. But Peter did not want anyone to think he had done this by his own power. He raised his voice so he could be heard over the murmuring throng.

"This man whom you see and know was made strong by the name of Jesus. Repent and turn to God so that your sins may be wiped out, that times of refreshing may come from the Lord. All the prophets from Samuel on have predicted these days. When God raised up his servant Jesus he sent him to bless you by turning each of you from your wicked ways. Repent! Repent!"

"THIS MAN WAS MADE STRONG BY THE NAME OF JESUS"

PETER

Peter's voice thundered in the street. The crowd grew larger still. As he looked into the faces of the people, Peter saw that their eyes were looking right past him. He heard the thumping of heavy footsteps behind him.

"Peter, the priests!" John called out.

Several priests, the captain of the temple guards, and some religious leaders broke through the crowd.

"What is going on here?" the captain's voice boomed. "Why are you causing all this commotion?"

"I am not causing any trouble," Peter answered. "I am simply telling the people about the Messiah."

"You are a fisherman. You are not a religious teacher," the priest objected. "It is not your place to teach about the Messiah."

"But I have seen him and known him. I cannot be silent."

The priest scoffed. "Ha! I know you. You're one of those followers of that carpenter from Nazareth."

"WHAT IS GOING ON HERE?"

PETER

"I am a follower of Jesus Christ, whom God has raised from the dead."

"This disturbance is unlawful," the temple guard insisted. "We must arrest you—you and your friend."

"But it is late in the day—"

The captain of the guard ignored Peter's protest. "Perhaps a night in jail will make you think twice about standing in the street outside the temple preaching blasphemy."

Abruptly the captain gave the signal and two guards pounced on Peter and John and twisted their arms behind them. They shoved John ahead of Peter.

"It's okay, Peter, " John said, calling over his shoulder to his companion. "God's power has been seen today. More have believed."

In fact, the number of believers grew to five thousand that day.

Peter and John were led off to jail.

"GOD'S POWER HAS BEEN SEEN TODAY"

HE HAD HARDLY SLEPT AT ALL

CHAPTER 10

Dawn came at last. The pinkish early morning light oozed through the small window high on the wall in the jail cell. Peter opened one eye and squinted at the light. With a groan, he pulled himself to an upright position and reached up to rub his aching shoulder. He had slept awkwardly. Actually, he had hardly slept at all, but the jail cell had no comfortable place to sit. All over his body, his muscles had grown stiff overnight. He turned his head from side to side to loosen his neck.

"John. Wake up." Peter nudged his snoring companion. "It's morning."

John jerked at Peter's touch. "What? Where are we?" John looked around. "Oh. Still here."

"I don't think we'll be here for long, though," Peter said.

"Why not?"

Peter shrugged. "They really have no charge against us."

"I'm not sure they need one, Peter. They usually get their way."

As if to reinforce John's point, the guard outside the cell paced with a heavy step, making sure his presence was known.

Peter was not discouraged. "I sat up praying most of the night. I do not believe we are in any danger."

The guard put the key in the lock and turned it. Roughly, he pulled the door open. "Breakfast," he said gruffly. He set a tray down on the cell's floor and shoved it with his foot, not caring that the food slid off the tray to the dirty floor. The door slammed shut again, the sound echoing off the stone walls.

"Thank you," John said to the guard, showing no response to the rude behavior.

"I wasn't hungry anyway," Peter said, looking away from the destroyed breakfast.

"I WASN'T HUNGRY ANYWAYS"

"I suppose it's better to face the Sanhedrin on an empty stomach."

"What are you so nervous about?"

"The Sanhedrin is the highest court in Israel," John said. "Our fate is in their hands—and they don't like us."

"We are in God's hands," Peter replied. "I told you we are in no danger."

"I pray not."

For a long time they did not speak. Each of them kept his thoughts to himself and murmured prayers under his breath.

Then the guard returned with several others. "It's time."

The door creaked as he yanked it open. He nodded toward Peter and John. "Take them."

The other temple guards seized them and shoved them forward, down the hall and out of the building.

Outside, Peter squinted at the sunlight—too bright

PETER SQUINTED AT THE SUNLIGHT

after the dark cell with only one small window. He knew where they were going and he knew the way. With his head held high, he walked toward the place where the Sanhedrin would be gathered, waiting for them.

Inside, Peter scanned the room. Annas, the high priest, was there, along with Caiphas, his son-in-law. Various other members of the high priest's family were there. The Sanhedrin was supposed to be the high court of Israel, representing rulers and teachers of the ancient Scriptures. But clearly the high priest had strong influence among this group.

In one corner stood the beggar they had healed the day before. Peter wondered if he had been held all night as well.

Peter glanced over at John, who had moved into place alongside Peter. John nodded ever so slightly to let Peter know that he believed they would be safe in God's hands.

ANNAS WAS THERE ALONG WITH CAIPHAS

A hush fell over the whole room. Annas cleared his throat. Peter and John looked at him squarely.

"By what power or what name did you heal that man yesterday?" He gestured toward the nervous beggar.

Peter felt the Holy Spirit rush through him. If he had even the slightest fear about speaking up before the Sanhedrin, it was banished. The high priest had asked him a question. He would answer it boldly and honestly.

"Rulers and elders of the people, we are being called to account today for an act of kindness. Know this: It is by the name of Jesus Christ of Nazareth, whom you crucified but whom God raised from the dead, that this man stands before you healed. Salvation is found in no one else, for there is no other name under heaven given to humans by which we must be saved."

The members of the Sanhedrin leaned in toward

"SALVATION IS FOUND IN NO ONE ELSE!"

each other and murmured. Peter could not hear their words, but he knew they were reacting to what he had just said. His speech, though short, was direct. He had clearly declared that Jesus was more powerful than any of these respected religious leaders.

"Simon Peter," said one of the priests somberly. "Where were you educated? At whose feet did you study?"

"I am an ordinary fisherman," Peter replied. "Many in this room are much more educated than I am, yet I speak the truth to you."

"You were with this Jesus of Nazareth?"

Peter nodded. "For three years I lived and walked and worked with him."

Once again the powerful men of Israel huddled together. Peter glanced over at John, who had not spoken but who also remained calmly confident.

After a few moments of hushed conversation, the members of the Sanhedrin faced Peter and John once

"I AM AN ORDINARY FISHERMAN"

again. "Remove the prisoners so that we may confer freely," Annas's voice boomed.

Peter and John were escorted outside the room. They leaned against the wall, side by side. The guard stood across from them, not caring what they might say to each other. They talked in hushed tones.

"You were right, Peter," John said. "They are having a hard time making a case against us. How can they possibly look down on a beggar who was healed. But they don't like our preaching, especially in the name of Jesus."

Peter shrugged. "By now everybody in Jerusalem knows what happened outside the temple gate yesterday," he said confidently. "It would be pointless for them to deny it."

"But they'll try to stop us," John said, shaking his head.

"They may want to, but they won't be able to."

"Even if they could, there are over five thousand

"THEY'LL TRY TO STOP US"

believers in Jerusalem now. More are believing every day."

Peter nodded in agreement. "This is much too big for the Sanhedrin to try to squelch. They're going to have to come face-to-face with the power of Jesus."

Abruptly a door opened and they were ushered back in and once again stood in the center of the room, all eyes on them.

"You are free to go," Annas said. "But you will not speak or teach in the name of Jesus ever again."

This time John spoke up. "Judge for yourselves whether it is right in God's sight for us to obey you rather than God."

Peter stared at Annas, free of all nervousness. "We cannot help speaking about what we have seen and heard."

"How dare you flaunt the authority of the Sanhedrin!" Caiphas growled at them. "If you speak in the name of Jesus, there will be consequences for

"HOW DARE YOU FLAUNT THE AUTHORITY OF THE SANHEDRIN!"

your actions! I warn you!"

Peter looked over at the healed man, who was still standing in the corner on two solid, healthy legs. There was the proof of the power of Jesus' name. People all over the city were praising God because of this miracle. The Sanhedrin had no authority over that.

With a respectful bow of his head, Peter turned to leave, with John close behind.

THE SANHEDRIN HAD NO AUTHORITY OVER THAT

"THE FOOD BASKETS ARE READY"

CHAPTER 11

"Joshua!" Peter called to one of the young believers who worked beside him every day. "The food baskets are ready." He tucked a last sack of grain into one basket and turned to the teenager who had promptly appeared when he called. "Here is some money. Stop in the market and buy some meat for these families."

"I know about the first three baskets," Joshua said, taking the coins from Peter and dropping them safely into a pouch. "But who is to get the fourth one?"

"The family that was in here yesterday with the three small children," Peter answered. "They're staying with relatives in a house over behind the temple. Just ask for Joseph; you'll find him."

Together Peter and Joshua loaded the heavy baskets onto a cart and hitched it to a donkey. This was the third trip Joshua had made that day. Soon they would have to recruit more help for deliveries.

Peter slapped the animal's backside, and the donkey reluctantly started moving forward. Mathias walked alongside, keeping an eye on the teetering baskets.

"Look out for any other believers who are in need." Peter called out one final instruction to the boy, who waved that he had heard. He knew he should do that anyway.

Peter took advantage of the chance to stand alone in the street for a few minutes enjoying the sense of satisfaction he felt. For weeks now, believers all over Jerusalem had been selling their property and possessions and contributing money to a common account. Peter and the other leaders used this fund to make sure all the believers had their basic needs met. No one was required to sell their property, and if they did, they could keep back some of the money

"LOOK OUT FOR OTHER BELIEVERS IN NEED!"

to take care of their own expenses. But Peter was overwhelmed at the generosity of the Christians. Actions like this could help spread the good news of Jesus through the whole city.

Along with the other disciples, Peter had continued to preach to anyone who would listen to him. He knew the Jewish leaders still did not like it. But he had promised to obey God, not humans, and he refused to stifle the truth. The whole world needed to hear about the resurrection of Jesus Christ. The new group of believers, the Church, would not just be in Jerusalem. This faith would spread around the globe, Peter was sure of it.

John and Andrew appeared from around the corner of the building, bringing Peter's moment of solitude to an end.

"Did Joshua go again already?" Andrew asked.

"Just a few moments ago."

"I found a family who has no place to stay. Their

THIS FAITH WOULD SPREAD AROUND THE GLOBE

relatives have kicked them out of the home because they have believed in Jesus."

"Then we will find them a new home," Peter said calmly.

"I heard that Ananias and Sapphira sold a piece of land and plan to contribute to the fund," John said.

Peter nodded. "I am expecting Ananias any moment now. He has pledged the full amount of the sale."

"I've seen the property. I'm sure he got a good price."

Peter wiped his forehead on his sleeve. "The sun is hot," he said. "Let's wait inside."

Only a few minutes later, Ananias appeared. With a broad smile on his bearded face, he took out a small leather pouch and turned it upside down on the table. A steady stream of gold coins tumbled out of the sack and clattered on the wooden table. "It is my pleasure to contribute the full price of my land to the

" I AM EXPECTING ANANIAS ANY MOMENT NOW "

apostles' fund. May you use this money as God
directs you."

Peter and the others smiled with satisfaction.
Curious onlookers gathered around the table and
looked at the money. It was an impressive contribu-
tion that would help a lot of people. Ananias beamed
and stood up straight.

With two fingers, Peter reached out and swiftly
pulled one coin toward him at a time, counting under
his breath. When the last coin was counted, he
looked up at Ananias, ready to thank him for his
generosity.

But something kept Peter from speaking those
words of thanks. A familiar presence overshadowed
his own mind and his thoughts turned in a completely
different direction. The smile on his face disappeared. Something was wrong. Ananias was lying.
This was not the full amount from the sale of the
land. Peter pushed the pile of money toward the

ANANIAS WAS LYING

center of the table.

"Ananias," he said, "how is it that Satan has so filled your heart that you have lied to the Holy Spirit and have kept for yourself some of the money you received for the land?"

He looked at Ananias's shocked expression. Surely Ananias wondered how Peter could possibly have known how much he had profited from the sale.

Peter shook his head sadly. No one required Ananias to give all of the money. Why should he lie and say that he did? He stood up and started pacing around the nervous Ananias.

Ananias was clearly rattled. "I...I..., well, I...."

When Peter spoke again, his voice thundered. "You have not just lied to me or to the other apostles or to all the believers. You have lied to God!"

Immediately Ananias dropped down to the floor. For a moment, the onlookers stood perfectly still, waiting for him to move or to say something. But

"I...I..., WELL, I..."

soon it was obvious he was dead.

Several young men stepped forward, wrapped up the body of Ananias in a blanket, and hurriedly carried him out.

Peter put his hand to his forehead, grieved at what had happened. Why had Ananias lied? Why? His wife Sapphira was supposed to come by that afternoon. Would she also lie?

For three hours, Peter tinkered with one task after another, not able to concentrate fully. If Ananias and Sapphira had succumbed to Satan's temptations, how many other new and tender believers would give in?

Finally Sapphira arrived. Peter met her at the table where he had left Ananias's money untouched.

"Is Ananias here?" she asked cheerily. "I was supposed to meet him here."

Peter gestured toward the pile of coins and the empty leather pouch. "Is this the price you and

IT WAS OBVIOUS HE WAS DEAD

Ananias got for the land?"

Sapphira bent over slightly to look closely at the money, calculating. "Yes," she said finally, "that is the price."

Peter rolled his eyes and turned away from her. "How could you agree to test the Spirit of the Lord?"

Sapphira jumped back, startled by his sudden thunderous attack.

Peter waved his hands toward the young men who had earlier carried away Ananias.

"Look, the feet of the men who buried your husband are at the door, and they will carry you out also."

Instantly, Sapphira fell down and died. The young men stepped forward and carried her out.

Those remaining in the room were silent. No one moved. Finally, Andrew stepped forward and put his hand on his brother's shoulders.

"HOW COULD YOU TEST THE SPIRIT OF THE LORD?!"

"Why did they do it?" Peter asked. "For the rest of my life I will never forget that moment when I knew that Ananias had lied and would have to die for it."

Andrew sighed. "Peter, the believers must know that they cannot deceive God, even when they deceive the rest of us."

Peter nodded. "I know, I know." He ran his hand through his thick dark beard. "Satan must not get hold of the Church."

"SATAN MUST NOT GET HOLD OF THE CHURCH"

THE MEDITERRANEAN WAS BEAUTIFUL

CHAPTER 12

Peter reached the top of the stairs leading up the side of the house to the roof. With one last tired step, he was safely on the flat roof of his friend's house in Joppa. From the roof, he could see the Mediterranean Sea. He was a long way from home, far from the familiar waters of the Sea of Galilee. He had not been fishing for a long time. The Mediterranean was beautiful, but he longed for home.

At least he had a friend in Joppa who would allow him to visit and rest. Ever since the Holy Spirit had entered him that day when he preached to a crowd of three thousand people in Jerusalem, Peter had constantly been out preaching and starting churches. He loved it; he would not trade it for his old life. But he was sometimes lonely for familiar things and the closeness of his family. He had come to this house, to this rooftop, seeking some quiet and a chance to pray without interruptions.

His friend's wife had promised to bring him some food in a few minutes. For now, he would just rest and enjoy the fresh air. He sank into a chair and gazed out at the blue sea.

Without meaning to, Peter began to pray silently. In another few minutes, he was completely absorbed in his prayer. But it was a different sort of prayer than he had ever experienced. He was not speaking words with his eyes closed. Rather, his eyes were wide open and he was seeing and hearing a vision right before his eyes. Any sense of drowsiness had passed; he was alert and attentive to what he was seeing.

The sky above split open and something like a large sheet was let down to earth by its four corners. The sheet held all kinds of four-footed animals, as well as reptiles and birds. The animals of this strange collection scrambled around noisily, cawing and

THE SKY ABOVE SPLIT OPEN

snorting and stamping their hooves. Peter recognized many of these animals as being unclean according to Jewish law. They were animals he had never touched or eaten. Why would he be seeing such a vision as he prayed?

His thoughts were broken by a voice speaking clearly, though no one else was with him on the roof. "Get up, Peter," the voice said. "Kill and eat."

Involuntarily Peter shrunk back from the vision. "Surely not, Lord!" he said. "I have never eaten anything impure or unclean."

But the voice spoke again. "Do not call anything made by God unclean."

Peter was not convinced. Though he was a believer in Jesus Christ, he considered himself a good Jew and obeyed the Jewish laws. How could he possibly consider eating an animal that the Scriptures taught were unclean?

But the voice persisted. Three times it repeated

"SURELY NOT, LORD!"

the command to kill and eat these animals and followed each command with the assurance that God had made all things clean. Then the sheet full of animals was taken back up in the air and the sky closed up.

Peter broke out into a sweat. What did this mean? He had come up to the roof for a simple afternoon of prayer, and instead he had encountered the voice of the Lord and strange commands. What was he supposed to do? Why had the Lord told him these things?

So absorbed in his own thoughts, Peter almost did not hear the commotion at the bottom of the stairs. It finally disrupted his thoughts. Leaning over the railing, he looked at the strangers who had appeared at his friend's door. He could not hear the whole conversation, but he heard his name mentioned repeatedly by the three strangers. Two of them looked like servants; the third was a Roman soldier.

WHY HAD THE LORD TOLD HIM THESE THINGS?

And then he heard another voice—the Lord speaking to him again. "Three men are looking for you. Go downstairs. Don't be afraid to go with them, for I have sent them to find you."

Peter responded immediately. His thunderous voice carried through the air and broke up the huddle at the foot of the stairs. "I am Peter," he called down. He started down the stairs. "I'm the one you are looking for. Why have you come?"

A soldier answered. "We have come from Cornelius the centurion. He is a righteous and God-fearing man who is respected by all the Jewish people. An angel told him to have you come to his house so he could hear what you have to say."

"Then I will come," Peter answered without hesitating. Surely this was connected to the vision he had just had. He still did not know what it meant, but all he could do was obey God one step at a time.

ALL HE COULD DO WAS OBEY GOD

PETER

They traveled for two days to reach Caesarea, on the northern end of Samaria, close to Galilee. During the dusty walk, Peter learned that Cornelius was a religious man who gave generously to people in need and prayed regularly. Two days earlier he had had a vision of an angel who told him to find Peter and bring him to his home.

Peter was confident that the two visions—his and Cornelius's—were connected. God was preparing both of them for this encounter. Though he sincerely believed in God, Cornelius was not a Jew; under normal circumstances Peter would not have anything to do with a Gentile. But these were not ordinary circumstances.

When they reached Cornelius' house, it was clear that the centurion had spent two days preparing for this visit. The house was full of friends and relatives. Servants buzzed about with dishes laden with rich foods. But at the sight of Peter, Cornelius lost

THESE WERE NOT ORDINARY CIRCUMSTANCES

interest in all the commotion. He fell at Peter's feet and wrapped himself around his ankles.

Peter touched the man's shoulders. "Please get up," he said, "I am only a man myself."

"Welcome to my home," Cornelius said, "and thank you for coming. We have gathered here because we want to hear what you have to say."

Peter looked at the eager crowd. He was used to speaking to Jewish crowds, where he could quote the prophets of centuries ago. This was different. These Romans would not know what the Jews knew. But it was clear to Peter now that God had brought him here to tell these people of God's love. Silently he prayed for the right words.

"You all know that it is against our law for a Jew to associate with a Gentile. But God has shown me that I should not call anything unclean. So when I was sent for, I came without any question.

"God accepts people from every nation if they

"GOD ACCEPTS PEOPLE FROM EVERY NATION"

fear him and do what is right. You know the message
that God sent to the people of Israel telling the good
news of peace through Jesus Christ, who is Lord of
all. You have heard what has happened throughout
Judea, beginning in Galilee. I can testify to you
about everything that Jesus of Nazareth did—teach-
ing and preaching and healing the sick. He was killed
by hanging on a wooden cross. But God raised him
from the dead on the third day, and he was seen by
many people. He told us to preach to the people and
to say that Jesus is the one whom God appointed as
judge of all people. All the prophets in the Scriptures
testified about him. Everyone who believes in him
receives forgiveness of sins."

All the busyness at the time of Peter's arrival had
passed. Everyone sat still and listened to what he had
to say. Even the servants huddled in the doorways
trying to hear him. Curious children stopped their
play to watch what was happening.

"EVERYONE WHO BELIEVES IN HIM RECEIVES FORGIVENESS"

"I do believe," Cornelius said boldly when Peter finally finished. "I do believe in this Jesus of Nazareth."

Others around the room were nodding that they believed also.

With fresh amazement at the ways of God, Peter realized that the good news about Jesus had spread way beyond Jerusalem and the Jewish people. Jesus had come to the Gentiles, too.

"I DO BELIEVE IN THIS JESUS OF NAZARETH"

THE HEAVY CHAINS CLANKED

CHAPTER 13

The heavy chains clanked as Peter tried to shift his weight and find a more comfortable position. It was hard to sleep weighed down by the chains and trapped between two soldiers, with two more standing guard outside the door. Every few hours a fresh set of soldiers replaced the ones who had been watching him. Peter had not had a good night's sleep for several days. In the morning he would face trial. Peter knew that this might be the end of his life.

King Herod, ruling over the Jewish people on behalf of the Roman government, was determined to squelch the growing Church. He had arrested dozens of believers. Then he had executed James. Peter's own heart was stabbed with fresh grief every time he thought about his good friend James being killed by a sword. But the Jewish leaders had been pleased with the king's action, so now Herod was after

PETER

Peter. He was only waiting until the religious holidays were over before executing Peter as well.

Peter's mind filled with images of the thousands of believers he had known. For most of a decade, Peter had been preaching about Jesus Christ and overseeing the work of the Church in Jerusalem. The Church had grown well beyond a small band of followers of Jesus. It was much bigger than even the three thousand people who had first seen the Holy Spirit come to the disciples. It was rapidly spreading throughout all the Jewish territories.

The Jewish leaders did not like this, and they had King Herod on their side. The room was dark. Peering through the shadows, Peter studied the face of the soldier on his left, a young man who was simply following orders. On his right was an older soldier who seemed annoyed at having to sit up half the night. When Peter had begun singing a couple of hours earlier, the gruff soldier had ordered him to be

PETER STUDIED THE FACE OF THE SOLDIER

silent. In the quiet Peter could occasionally hear the shuffling feet of the two soldiers at their posts outside the door.

Leaning his head back and sighing, Peter closed his eyes and began to pray. As long as he did not make any noise, the irritated soldier could not object to that. Eventually Peter drifted off to sleep.

After a while he felt someone nudging him. "I'm not making a sound," Peter said in his own defense. He kept his eyes closed, trying to recapture the precious moments of sleep.

Again he felt someone swat the side of his body. This time Peter sat bolt upright. Through the darkness of the cell shone a beam of light. Peter looked closely for the source—and saw an angel. It was the angel who had nudged him awake.

His heart racing, Peter looked at the two guards on either side of him. Though awake, they seemed not to see the angel. Yet he was sure he was not

PETER LOOKED — AND SAW AN ANGEL

dreaming; perhaps it was a vision, like the one he had seen when the Lord sent him to Cornelius.

"Quick, get up," the angel said. He touched Peter again, and the chains fell off his wrists.

Peter started rubbing his sore wrists, still looking around the room for the guards to react.

"Put on your clothes and your sandals," the angel said. "Wrap your cloak around you and follow me."

The angel was already starting to leave the room. Peter scrambled into his clothes and chased after the beam of light. He felt as if he were watching himself in action. The soldiers did not move. They did not even turn their heads.

Peter followed the angel right past the second set of guards, who made no movement. They seemed not to even see Peter going by. In a few minutes, Peter and the angel were safely outside the prison building. Not one person had tried to stop them.

Peter followed the angel till they came to the iron

"QUICK, GET UP"

gate leading into the city. To his amazement, it opened for them all by itself and they walked right through it. Peter's mind was full of questions, but the angel had not spoken since they left the prison. Peter followed, trancelike, as the angel led him up the street.

Suddenly the angel left.

Peter was fully awake now. This was no dream. And it was no vision. An angel of the Lord had come and released him from prison before Herod could execute him.

"My work is not done," Peter said to himself. "The Lord has rescued me so that I can serve him more." He was saved from Herod's clutches. Everything that the Jewish leaders were expecting to happen simply would not happen.

Peter looked around to get his bearings and then headed off in the direction of his friend, Mary. He knew believers had been gathered there for days

PETER FOLLOWED, TRANCE-LIKE

praying for him. It was the middle of the night, but he went anyway. The streets were empty, but Peter hurried to get out of sight. What if the guards should suddenly realize he was gone and come looking for him?

Finally he reached Mary's house. He banged on the door with his fist. No one answered. He pounded again.

A servant girl named Rhoda came to the door.

"Who is there?" she called without opening the door.

"It's me!" Peter answered.

Instead of hearing the locks turning to let him in, Peter heard Rhoda's footsteps moving away from the door. She disappeared into the house.

Peter raised his hand to knock again. This time he did not stop until the door was opened.

"Hello, friends," he said with a wide grin on his face.

"IT'S ME"

PETER

The faces that looked back at him were frozen with astonishment. Obviously they could not believe their eyes. Was this really Peter?

At last someone grabbed Peter's arm and pulled him into the house.

"When Rhoda said it was you, we couldn't believe it." They closed the door solidly behind him.

"You've been praying for me, haven't you?" Peter said. "Why should you be so surprised when God answers your prayers?"

The house, quiet a few minutes ago, buzzed with excitement now. The believers had more questions than Peter could answer. Finally, he raised his hands to silence them and told them the whole story, from the moment he saw the angel until he reached the door a few minutes ago.

"We are thrilled to see you safe, but you can't stay here, Peter," someone said somberly.

Peter nodded. "I know. I just wanted you all to

"WHY SHOULD YOU BE SO SURPRISED...?"

know about the miracle. Tell the others about it as soon as you can."

"Sooner or later those soldiers will discover you're missing," a voice urged. "They've been watching this house. You must go!"

"Yes, yes, I will." Peter looked at the group tenderly. He did not want to leave them. But he had no choice. If the soldiers found him here in the morning, everyone would be in danger. He could not risk that.

Peter pulled the wooden door open and stepped outside. In another moment, alone again, he had disappeared into the darkness.

HE HAD NO CHOICE

"WILL AN ANGEL RELEASE YOU FROM THIS PRISON?"

CHAPTER 14

Peter tilted the jug straight upside down, hoping for just a bit more of the liquid. All this talking had left him very thirsty. But the jug was empty.

The young man had long ago scooted his chair up close to the old man to hear every word he said. The candle on the table between them burned low, casting shadows against the walls.

"Do you think an angel will release you from this prison?" the young man asked, gesturing around the room.

"I do not know. If the Lord again sends an angel to rescue me, then I will know that I still have work to do." Peter ran his fingers through his beard thoughtfully. His voice dropped almost to a whisper. "But if no angel comes, if this is the end of my life, then I can go to my Lord knowing that I have done all I could to let the world know of the power of Christ." He stood up and turned away from the boy.

"Perhaps I can help you escape," the young man offered eagerly.

Peter looked over his shoulder at the teenager and raised an eyebrow. "So you believe?"

Scraping his chair on the bare floor as he pushed it back, the young man rose to his feet and went to stand facing Peter. "How could I not believe? The stories you have told, the experiences you have had—no one would risk so much for something that was not the absolute truth."

Peter smiled. "If you truly believe, then even my imprisonment has not been in vain. I can die knowing I served my Lord right up to the end."

"But I can help you get out," the boy insisted.

For a fraction of a second, Peter considered the offer. Then he shook his head. "No. I have no wish to endanger you for my own sake. I am prepared for whatever may happen."

The young man looked out the window. "It will be dawn soon."

"SO YOU BELIEVE ?"

Peter nodded. "And they will come for me. This is the day I am to face trial."

"But you have done nothing wrong!"

Peter stepped to the window. The orange hues of the morning sun were seeping through the spaces between the proud buildings of Rome. In another hour or so the city would be bustling with life. And Peter's life could very well be over before the day was done. He turned to face the boy.

"Young man, when you came in with my dinner you asked if I was afraid to die."

The boy nodded. "And you said no."

"And I still say no. But I hope that now you understand why I said that."

"I think I do."

"I am an old man. I have given my life to preaching about Jesus, starting churches, especially among the Jews, consulting with other leaders as we tried to sort out the difficulties that have come up over the years. It was not our purpose to begin a new religion.

"YOU ASKED IF I WAS AFRAID TO DIE"

but to announce the fulfillment of the old one. Nevertheless, the Church was born and it has needed tending. So have I tended it. I have fed the sheep."

He paused for a moment and looked at the boy's puzzled expression.

"Let me get to the point," Peter said. "I am an old man. But you are a young man. Perhaps it is now your turn to be a leader—you and others like you who really believe."

"But I am young," the boy protested, "and untrained. I know so little. I cannot be a leader."

Peter nodded. "I, too, said all those things at one time. And they were all true. But that did not stop God then, and it will not stop God now. His power is mightier than any fear you have."

The young man had grown quiet and simply nodded. He did not fully understand, but he was sincere in his simple belief.

They both turned their heads as they heard the door opening. The soldiers had come for Peter.

THE SOLDIERS HAD COME FOR PETER

AWESOME BOOKS FOR KIDS!

The Young Reader's Christian Library
Action, Adventure, and Fun Reading!

This series for young readers ages 8 to 12 is action-packed, fast-paced, and Christ-centered! With exciting illustrations on every other page following the text, kids won't be able to put these books down! Over 100 illustrations per book. All books are paperbound. The unique size (4 ¾₆" x 5 ¾") makes these books easy to take anywhere!

A Great Selection to Satisfy All Kids!